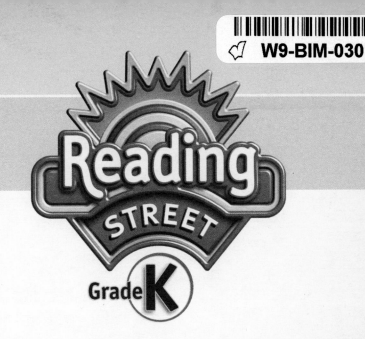

Scott Foresman

Practice Book 6

Teacher's Manual

Unit 6

PEARSON
Scott Foresman

Editorial Offices: Glenview, Illinois • Parsippany, New Jersey • New York, New York
Sales Offices: Needham, Massachusetts • Duluth, Georgia • Glenview, Illinois
Coppell, Texas • Sacramento, California • Mesa, Arizona

ISBN: 0-328-14529-7

2 3 4 5 6 7 8 9 10 V004 09 08 07 06 05

Contents

Unit 6
Building Our Homes

	Family Times	Phonics	High-Frequency Words	Phonics Story	Comprehension	Grammar
Homes Around the World	1–2	3, 8	4	5–6	7, 9	10
Old MacDonald Had a Woodshop	11–12	13, 18	14	15–16	17, 19	20
Building Beavers	21–22	23, 28	24	25–26	27, 29	30
The Night Worker	31–32	33, 38	34	35–36	37, 39	40
The House That Tony Lives In	41–42	43, 48	44	45–46	47, 49	50
Animal Homes	51–52	53, 58	54	55–56	57, 59	60

Help Sam find his way home by following the path of /a/ pictures.

Family Times

You are your child's first teacher!

This week we're ...

Reading *Homes Around the World*

Talking About Homes Around the World

Learning About Phonics Review
Compare and Contrast

Here are ways to help your child practice skills while having fun!

Day 1 **Read Together**

Describe an item in the house with an /a/ or an /i/. Have your child guess the item. For example, say, *I am thinking of a paper that shows the roads and cities.* The answer is a *map.* Take turns giving clues and guessing the objects.

Day 2 **Read Together**

Have your child read the Phonics Story *Vin and the Bag.* Find /a/ and /i/ words.

Day 3 **Short Vowels**

Read the following words to your child. Have your child tell you whether the word has an /a/ or an /i/.

bat   pit   Jim   man

Day 4 **Words That Describe Action**

Ask your child to name some verbs. Tell your child that the letter *s* needs to be added when the verb is used with some words: *He runs. Bob walks. She skips.* Have your child give some sentences with action words that need *s.*

Day 5 **Practice Handwriting**

Have your child write the following /a/ and /i/ words.

sat   sit   fan   fin

Words to talk about

home	roof	tools
apartment	city	country

Words to read

where	come	what
little	from	that
jam	van	mix
quit	hill	bag

Name _____

 **Write**    **Color**

m a t

c a b

p i g

Aa
Ii

p i n

k i t

j a m

 Directions: Name each picture. Write *a* or *i* to finish each word. Color the /a/ pictures.

 Home Activity: Have your child write *tin* and *tan* and color a picture for each word.

Practice Book Unit 6

Phonics Review **3**

Name _____

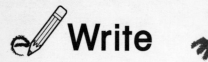 Write  Color

| where | with | they | like |

_____

 **They** play with a ball.

_____

 **Where** do you live?

_____

I will go **with** you.

_____

I **like** to run fast.

 Directions: Write the missing words to finish each sentence. Color the pictures.

 Home Activity: Have your child use the high-frequency words in other sentences.

4 **High-Frequency Words**

Vin will zip the bag.

He and the bag will go on a trip.

4

Vin and the Bag

Vin had a bag.

The bag is a big bag.

1

He got one big can.

He got one little net.

He got one little kit.

He got one big rag.

Name _____

 Color

 Directions: Color the picture that is different.

 Home Activity: Have children tell how the pictures are alike and how they are different.

Name _____

 Circle   Color

lid  lad		pin pan	
fan fin		crib crab	

 Directions: Circle the word that names the picture.
Color the /i/ pictures.

 Home Activity: Have your child draw a picture of
something with /i/.

Name _____

 Color

 Directions: Color the pictures that are alike.

 Home Activity: Have your child tell how the pictures are alike and how they are different.

Practice Book Unit 6

Comprehension Compare and Contrast **9**

Name _____

 Circle  Write

sit

sits

The dog __**sits**__ .

hop

hops

The frog **hops** .

mop

mops

Will can **mop** .

pet

pets

She **pets** the cat.

hit

hits

Jill can **hit** it.

cut

cuts

He **cuts** the bun.

 Directions: Circle the correct word to finish the
sentence. Write the word on the line.

 School + Home **Home Activity:** Have children read each sentence.

10 **Grammar** Verbs That Add -s

Practice Book Unit 6

Color the /o/ pictures. Draw lines to the matching rhyming words.

Family Times

You are your child's first teacher!

This week we're ...

Reading *Old MacDonald had a Woodshop*

Talking About Building Things

Learning About Phonics Review
Character

4

1

Here are ways to help your child practice skills while having fun!

Day 1 **Read Together**

Write _op on a sheet of paper. Ask your child to make words by adding a letter to -op. After many words are written, have your child say or write sentences using several of the rhyming words.

Day 2 **Read Together**

Have your child read the Phonics Story *Spin the Top*. Find /o/ words.

Day 3 **Short Vowels**

Tell your child that the first and last letters of these words are the same. Have him or her figure out the words.

_o_ (mom)   _o_ (pop)   _o_ (Bob)

Day 4 **Adjectives**

Have your child choose a story character in a book. Ask your child to talk about the character using words such as *brave girl, funny monkey,* or *fuzzy bunny.* Tell your child that he or she is using describing words.

Day 5 **Practice Handwriting**

Have your child get his or her favorite movie or book. Ask your child to copy down the title on a sheet of paper.

Words to talk about

| saw | drill | hammer |
| screwdriver | file | chisel |

Words to read

yellow	five	with
go	look	he
pot	mom	stop
top	box	rock

Name _____

 Write    **Color**

l o g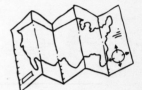

A a

m a p

t o p

I i

s o c k

h i l l

O o

p o t

 Directions: Write *a*, *i*, or *o* to finish each word. Color the /o/ pictures.

 Home Activity: Have your child write *lock* and *rock* and draw a picture for each word.

Name _____

 **Write**  **Color**

| what said was come |

_____

I will  **come** with you.

_____

I _____ **said** _____ I will run fast.

_____

What can I do to help?

_____

I _____ **was** _____ the best one for the job.

 Directions: Write the missing word to finish each sentence. Color the pictures.

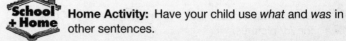 **Home Activity:** Have your child use *what* and *was* in other sentences.

14 **High-Frequency Words**

Dad will spin the top.

Dad can spin it.

Dad can get the top to spin.

4

Spin the Top

Bob got a top.

Bob will spin the top.

1

The top will not spin.

The top will not go.

Help! Help!

Help me spin the top.

It will not spin.

Help! Help!

Name _____

 Color 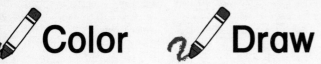 Draw

  **room of house**

  **woodshop**

 Directions: Color the pictures. Then draw a picture that tells setting of the story in the last box.

 Home Activity: Have your child draw a picture of the setting for one of his or her favorite stories.

Name _____

 Circle  Color

| top / tap | (top image) | hot / hat | (hat image) |
| lock / lick | (lock image) | cob / cab | (corn image) |

Directions: Circle the word that names the picture. Color the /o/ pictures.

School + Home **Home Activity:** Have your child draw a picture of something with /o/.

Draw Write

Directions: Draw your favorite scene from *Old MacDonald had a Woodshop*, then write or dictate words describing where and when it happened.

School + Home **Home Activity:** Talk about the favorite scene your child drew and what the setting is.

Name _____

 Circle  Write

 top

big

_____

The **big** dog is here.

 little

big

_____

The **little** cat ran.

 hat

fat

_____

One **fat** hen is here.

 sad

bad

_____

The **bad** dog got it.

 wet

get

_____

The **wet** pet is mad.

one

two

_____

One cat ran to the man.

Directions: Circle the adjective that matches the picture. Write the word to complete the sentence.

School + Home Home Activity: Have your child read each sentence.

20 **Grammar** Adjectives

Color the /e/ pictures. Draw lines to match the rhyming words.

Family Times

You are your child's first teacher!

This week we're ...

Reading *Building Beavers*

Talking About Animals Build

Learning About Phonics Review
Main Idea

Here are ways to help your child practice skills while having fun!

Day 1 **Read Together**

Have your child draw a picture of the word that rhymes with *fell* and begins with the letter *b*. Continue with *jet* and the letter *n,* and *peg* and the letter *l*.

Day 2 **Read Together**

Have your child read the Phonics Story *Jim and Kim.* Find words that have /e/.

Day 3 **Short Vowels**

Make a chart with /a/, /e/, /i/, and /o/. Have your child choose a book. Read through the story together. Write the words with /a/, /e/, /i/, and /o/ on the chart. Read the lists with our child.

Day 4 **Sentences**

Have your child use sentences to tell about his or her favorite game. Give these examples: *My favorite game is soccer. I play it at the park. I play with my friends.* Have your child use complete sentences to tell about his or her favorite game or toy.

Day 5 **Practice Handwriting**

Have your child copy the following sentence.

I can write and spell.

Words to talk about

beaver	lodge	paddle
stream	river	lake

Words to read

blue	she	three
are	do	here
pen	let	bell
get	fed	yes

Name _____

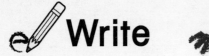 Write    Color

_____
w e b

_____
l e g

_____
p i n

Aa
Ee
Ii

_____
h a t

_____
m e n

_____
j e t

 Directions: Write *a*, *i*, or *e* to finish each word. Color the /e/ pictures.

 Home Activity: Have your child write *hen* and *pen* and draw a picture for each word.

Name _____

 Write  Color

| from | go | her | five |

_____

This is _____ **her** _____ big pet.

_____

I see _____ **five** _____ .

_____

The box is _____ **from** _____ him.

_____

I can _____ **go** _____ with you.

 Directions: Write the missing word to finish each sentence. Color the pictures.

 Home Activity: Use *five* and *from* in other sentences.

The hen had little ones.

Jim and Kim have lots of little hens.

4

Jim and Kim

Jim and Kim had a pet.

They had a pet hen.

The hen was in a pen.

1

Jim had fun with the pet hen.

Jim fed the hen.

Kim had fun with the pet hen.

Kim got a nest for the hen.

 **Circle**

pets

tools

homes

 Directions: Circle the word that tells what the pictures are all about.

 Home Activity: Have children tell about each picture.

Name _____

Name _____

 Circle  Color

net not		bad bed	
tan ten	10	pot pet	

 Directions: Circle the word that names the picture. Color the /e/ pictures.

School + Home **Home Activity:** Have your child draw a picture of something with /e/.

Name _____

 Circle  Color

pets

animals

plants

animals

Directions: Circle the word that tells what each picture is all about. Color the pictures.

 Home Activity: Have your child tell what the pictures are all about.

Name _____

 Write  Color

is   big   flag   the

_____

The flag is big.

a   has   pet   he

_____

He has a pet.

on   sits   she   a   box

_____

She sits on a box.

run   fast   can   I

_____

I can run fast.

Directions: Use the words in each box to write a telling sentence about the picture. Remember to use an uppercase letter and a period. Color the pictures.

 School + Home **Home Activity:** Have children read each sentence.

Color the boxes with /u/ pictures. What letter do you see?

Family Times

You are your child's first teacher!

This week we're ...

Reading *The Night Worker*

The Night Worker
Kate Banks Pictures by Georg Hallensleben

Talking About Building at Night

Learning About Phonics Review
Plot

Here are ways to help your child practice skills while having fun!

Day 1 **Read Together**

Tell your child to jump every time you say a /u/ word. Read the following sentences to your child.

The bug runs with the duck.
The cub hunts with the pup.

Day 2 **Read Together**

Have your child read the Phonics Story *Gus and the Bug*. Find /u/ words.

Day 3 **Short Vowels**

Have your child look around the house and find items that have /u/. Ask him or her to use the name of each item in a sentence.

Day 4 **Questions**

Remind your child that sentences can tell something or ask something. Review what a question is with these examples: *What time is dinner? Can I play a game?* Take turns asking and answering questions with your child.

Day 5 **Practice Handwriting**

Write, *What is your name?* on a sheet of paper. Have your child respond to the question by writing the question and then writing the answer in the form of a sentence.

Words to talk about

engineer **construction** **foreman**
hard hat **beacons**
street sweeper

Words to read

two	we	they
have	see	of
nut	fun	cup
cut	mug	bus

Name _____

 Write    Color

s u n

c u p

Aa

Oo

Uu

b u s

b a t

p u p

c o t

 Directions: Write *a, o,* or *u* to finish each word.
Color the /u/ pictures.

 Home Activity: Have your child write *hut* and *nut* and
draw a picture for each word.

Name _____

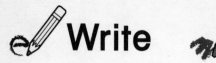 Write  Color

| are   that   yellow   do |

Did you see __**that**__ ?

The sun is __**yellow**__ .

__**Do**__ you like to jump?

Where __**are**__ you?

 Directions: Write the missing words to finish each sentence. Color the pictures.

 Home Activity: Have your child use the high-frequency words in other sentences.

Gus grabs the bug.

Gus lets the bug go.

4

Gus and the Bug

Gus will hug his mom.

Gus gets on the bus.

I

Gus sat with his pal Wes.

The sun was hot.

A bug got on the bus.

It sat with Gus and Wes.

Name _____

 Color

 Directions: Color the picture that shows what would happen next in each story.

 Home Activity: Have your child tell you the story of *The Night Worker*.

Name _____

 Circle  Color

net nut 	(walnut)	cut cat	(cat)
cub cob	(dog)	rug rag	(rug)

 Directions: Circle the word that names the picture.
Color the /u/ pictures.

 Home Activity: Have your child draw a picture of
something with /u/.

Name _____

 Draw

🍎 **Directions:** Draw a picture to show what would happen next in each story.

 Home Activity: Ask your child to recall what happened after school today, telling the events in order.

Comprehension Plot **39**

Name _____

✏️ Draw

Where is the cat?

Do you see the dog?

What did the bug do?

Can you see me?

The bug ran to see me.

I can not see you.

The cat is here.

I can see the dog.

 Directions: Draw a line from each question to its answer.

School + Home **Home Activity:** Ask your child the questions and have him or her create an answer.

Write the letter for the vowel sound in each picture name.

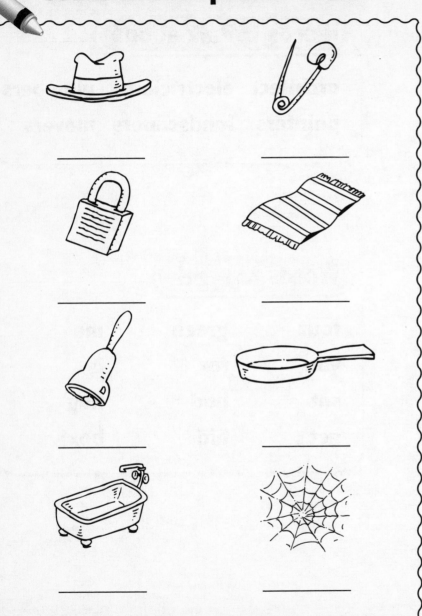

Family Times

You are your child's first teacher!

This week we're ...

Reading   *The House That Tony Lives In*

The HOUSE That TONY Lives IN

By Anthony Lorenz   Illustrated by John Sandford

Talking About   Building a Home

Learning About   Phonics Review
Setting

Here are ways to help your child practice skills while having fun!

Day 1

Read Together

Show your child a picture. Ask your child to tell about the picture. When your child uses short vowel words, ask him or her to identify the vowel sound: /a/, /e/, /i/, /o/, or /u/.

Day 2

Read Together

Have your child read the Phonics Story *What Pets Do.* Point to various words and have your child say the word and identify the vowel sound.

Day 3

Short Vowels

Write the following word parts on a sheet of paper. Have your child write consonants and vowels to make new words.

_ _ n   _e _   p_t

Day 4

Exclamations

Write the exclamation mark on a sheet of paper and show it to your child. Tell your child that to show excitement, the exclamation mark is used. Give some examples such as *Wow! Bam!* and *Watch out!* Ask your child to give other examples.

Day 5

Practice Handwriting

Have your child write these sentences to practice using the exclamation mark.

Oh!   Wow!   Look at that!   Stop it!

2

Words to talk about

architect	electricians	plumbers
painters	landscapers	movers

Words to read

four	green	me
you	for	is
sat	had	hug
get	hid	box

Name _____

 Circle  Color

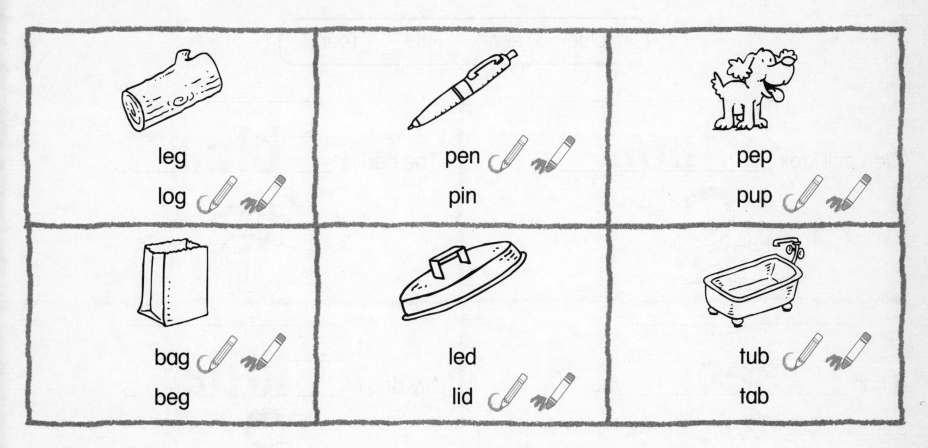

leg

log

pen

pin

pep

pup

bag

beg

led

lid

tub

tab

 Directions: Circle the word that names the picture.
Color the pictures.

 Home Activity: Have your child use the words in
sentences.

Practice Book Unit 6

Phonics Review **43**

Name _____

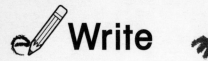 Write  Color

| blue | see | little | four |

_____

Do I still look **four** ?

_____

The bed is **blue** .

_____

I can **see** you.

_____

My dog is **little** .

Directions: Write the missing word to finish each sentence. Color the pictures.

 School + Home **Home Activity:** Have your child use the high-frequency words in other sentences.

Sam is a cat.

Sam will sit in a lap.

He will nap.

4

What Pets Do

Peg is a dog.

She will tug.

She will dig.

1

Hal is a pet pig.

He will run in his pen.

He will go in the mud.

Tad is a pet frog.

He will hop.

He will swim.

Name _____

 Color

MOVING
VAN

 Directions: Color the picture that shows the setting
of the story *The House That Tony Lives In*.

 School + Home **Home Activity:** Have your child tell you when and
where the story takes place.

Name _____

 Write  Color

f a n

c r a b

m a n

d e sk

pan

can

 Directions: Write the missing letter in each word. Color pictures that rhyme.

 Home Activity: Have your child use the picture names in sentences.

48 **Phonics** Review

Practice Book Unit 6

Name _____

 Color

 Directions: Color the picture that shows the setting for a story about the people helping to build a barn.

 Home Activity: Have your child tell where and when the story takes place.

Practice Book Unit 6

Comprehension Setting **49**

Name _____

 **Circle**

Can I swim?

Yes I can! !

She has a big dog! !

Pet the dog.

The pig is big.

I am glad! !

Is he sad?

Help me! !

 Directions: Circle the exclamation in each pair of sentences.

School +Home **Home Activity:** Have your child read each sentence.

50 **Grammar** Exclamations

Name the pictures. Draw lines to the vowel sound.

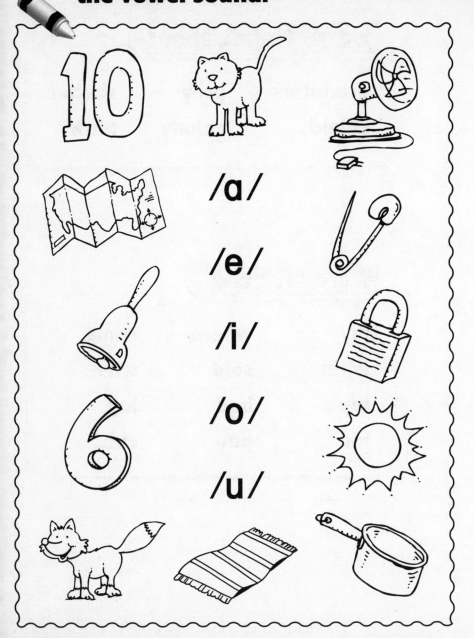

/a/

/e/

/i/

/o/

/u/

Family Times

You are your child's first teacher!

This week we're ...

> **Reading** *Animal Homes*

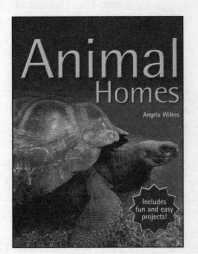

Talking About Building Animal Homes

Learning About Phonics Review
Draw Conclusions

Here are ways to help your child practice skills while having fun!

Day 1

Read Together

Have your child choose a book. Read through the story together and point out words with short vowel sounds.

Day 2

Read Together

Have your child read the Phonics Story *What Can You Do?* After reading, make a list of words with /a/, /e/, /i/, /o/, and /u/.

Day 3

Short Vowels

Write the rhyme *fox in a box* on a sheet of paper. Read the rhyme together and have your child identify the rhyming words. Help your child make other rhymes such as *cat in the hat, hen in a pen,* or *bug on a rug.*

Day 4

Complete Sentences

Tell your child the difference between giving short answers and using complete sentences. Explain that a complete sentence has a *naming part* and an *action part.* Have your child tell about school today using complete sentences.

Day 5

Practice Handwriting

Have your child answer the question using a complete sentence. Help him or her write the answer.

Question: What game do you like best?

Answer: I like . . . _____

2

Words to talk about

predators	prey	shelter
shields	colony	bark

Words to read

my	where	come
what	said	was
top	bed	lap
hit	pan	cub

3

Name _____

✏️ **Draw**

pin

pen

pan

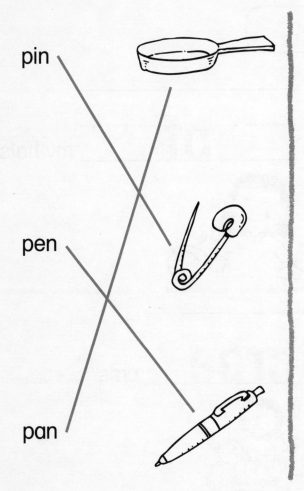

cub

cab

cob

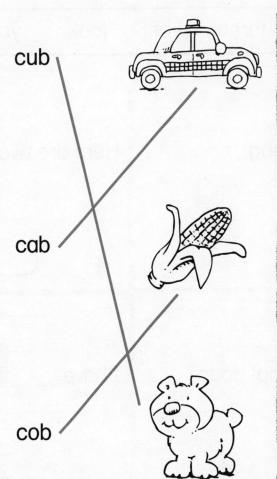

hut

hat

hit

 Directions: Draw lines to match the words with the pictures.

 School + Home **Home Activity:** Have your child draw pictures for these words: *cat, cot, cut.*

Name _____

 **Write**    **Color**

three	of	look	you

_____

Look at that bug.

_____

Here are two **of** my hats.

_____

Do **you** like hot dogs?

_____

I have **three** cats.

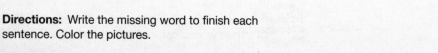 **Directions:** Write the missing word to finish each sentence. Color the pictures.

 Home Activity: Have your child use the high-frequency words in other sentences.

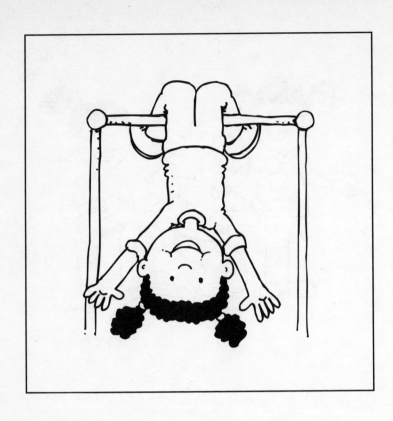

I am Jen.

I can hang from my legs.

What can you do?

4

What Can You Do?

Here is Ned.

Ned can run fast.

Ned can run and run.

1

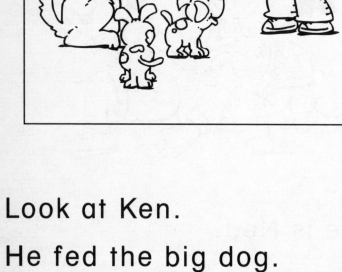

Look at Ken.

He fed the big dog.

He fed the little dogs.

2

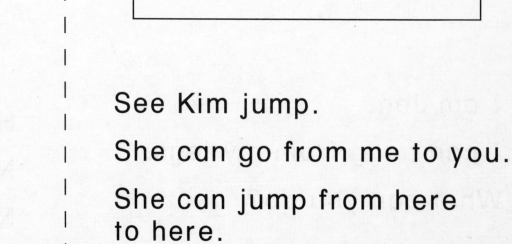

See Kim jump.

She can go from me to you.

She can jump from here
to here.

3

Name _____

 **Circle**

 Directions: Look at the animal home. Which animal would live in this home? Circle the animal.

 Home Activity: Have your child explain how he or she arrived at his or her conclusion.

Practice Book Unit 6

Comprehension Draw Conclusions **57**

Name _____

 **Write**

_____

cat

_____

cot

_____

bag

_____

bug

_____

pin

_____

pen

_____

net

_____

nut

 Directions: Write the word for each picture name.

 School + Home **Home Activity:** Have your child write *mop* and *map* and draw a picture for each word.

Name _____

 Circle  Color

mad

She is _____.   sad

glad

mad

He is _____.   sad

glad

Directions: Circle the word to finish the sentence that tells how the person would feel. Color the pictures.

Home Activity: Have your child tell why he or she drew the conclusion he or she did.

Practice Book Unit 6

Name _____

 Draw

The big dog

One doll

The man

A little pig

was on the bed.

had a little pup.

sat in the mud.

sat in the den.

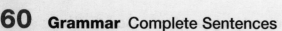 **Directions:** Draw lines to make complete sentences.

 Home Activity: Ask your child to make a new sentence using the sentence parts on the page.

60 Grammar Complete Sentences